From New York to California

by Lydia Bellochio
Illustrated by Linda Prater

Glenview, Illinois • Boston, Massachusetts • Mesa, Arizona
Shoreview, Minnesota • Upper Saddle River, New Jersey

Karina Otero just moved to California. She already misses her home in New York. She misses the buildings and her school.

She also misses her friends.

She misses the winter snow, most of all!

"Grandma," Karina asked, "why did we have to move here? I miss my friends and our home."

"Well, Karina," Grandma said, "we have more opportunities here than back home. And our family is here too. Don't you want to meet your cousins?"

Karina studied the wrinkles on Grandma's face. She knew Grandma was wise. She always gave her good advice.

Grandma gave Karina a hug. Her hugs were always reassuring. Karina was feeling better.

Karina helped Grandma move some boxes into the new apartment.

That night, Karina had a dream about meeting her relatives. She thought of all the picnics and parties they would go to together.

She wondered what her cousins were like. "I hope they like me," she thought. "I could use some friends here."

The next day, Karina and Grandma visited Aunt Lety and her family.

"Welcome to California, Karina" Aunt Lety said. "These are your cousins, Ariel and Angélica. I'm sure the three of you will be great friends!"

baseball

Karina went into the living room with her cousins. "Do you like baseball?" Ariel asked.

Karina had never played baseball before, but she tried anyway. The three of them went out to the back yard and threw the ball around.

Karina swung her bat and hit the ball out of the yard. "Wow!" Angélica said. "You moved the bat really fast. Next time, you'll be on my team!"

Karina was happy. Before she missed the snow and her friends in New York. But now she was starting to like it here in California.